JEWISH INSIGHTS
INTO SCRIPTURE

Eli Lizorkin-Eyzenberg, PhD

ISBN-13: 978-1981822041

Jewish Insights Into Scripture, Copyright © 2019 by Eliyahu Lizorkin-Eyzenberg. This book contains material protected under International and Federal Copyright Laws and Treaties. Any unauthorized reprint or use of this material is prohibited. No part of this book may be reproduced or transmitted in any form or by any means, electronic or mechanical, including photocopying, recording, or by any information storage and retrieval system without express written permission from the author (dr.eli.israel@gmail.com).

Contents

INTRODUCTION — 5

THE HEBREW TORAH

Don't Mess with Abraham! — 6

The Blessing Meant for Jacob — 7

Was Tamar a Saint or a Sinner (or Both)? — 9

A Match Made in Heaven — 10

JESUS IN HIS JEWISH CONTEXT

"First Let Me Bury My Father" — 12

"Unless You Hate Your Father and Mother…" — 14

"Unless Your Righteousness Surpasses..." — 16

What Did Jesus Teach about Divorce? — 18

Did Jesus Build "Fences" around the Torah? — 19

Did Jesus Declare All Foods Clean? — 21

Did Jesus Know the Future? — 23

Was Mary Magdalene Ever a Prostitute? — 25

Why Could Mary Not Touch Jesus? — 27

The Lion of the Tribe of Judah — 29

"If You Are the Messiah, Tell Us Clearly!"   30

BELIEVERS IN THE MESSIAH – THEN AND NOW

How New Is the New Covenant?   31

Who Was the First Comforter?   33

Who Said to Hold All Things in Common?   35

Did the Apostles Believe in the Trinity?   37

Did Shimon Peter Live as a Gentile?   39

Was the *Shema* Important to Paul?   41

Paul's Forgotten Rule   44

Was Paul Right about Women?   46

Did Paul Instruct Timothy to Eat Unclean Food?   49

Why Was Paul Against Circumcision?   51

The Law of Moses and the Grace of God   53

The Gospel in the Hebrew Bible   55

Torah and the Apostle Paul   57

Is There One Law for Everyone?   59

Gentile Christians and the Jewish Torah   61

Are Christians Now Jews?   63

Why Don't (All) Jews Believe in Jesus?   65

Luther, Hitler, and the Jews   67

Will the Temple Be Rebuilt?   69

REVELATION: THE APOCALYPSE OR UNVEILING

What Is the "Lord's Day"?   71

What Was the Throne of Satan?   73

666 or 616?   74

What Was the Mark of the Beast?   76

What Is Armageddon?   78

Who are the Seven Spirits?   80

THE HEBREW LANGUAGE AND JEWISH CULTURE

The Challenge of Translation   83

Can Work Be Worship?   85

The Biblical Hebrew Compass   86

The Hebrew Hallelujah   88

What Does Prayer Mean in Hebrew?   90

What We Think We Know   92

Grace in Judaism   94

Thank You for Not Making Me a Woman   96

Benjamin Netanyahu's Name   98

Introduction

In this short book you will find essays offering insights into Scripture from a Jewish perspective. Based on an understanding of the Hebrew language and the relevant historical contexts, the essays in this book raise questions of interest to modern believers in the Jewish Christ (Messiah).

I propose some answers that are consistent with the known textual and archaeological evidence as well as valuable recent contributions to Biblical interpretation. The writing is designed to be accessible for every reader, even if sometimes dealing with specific or even technical matters. It is my sincere hope that these insights will bless you as you continue in your quest to understand the Bible and live a faithful life of honoring Israel's God. Come learn more with us at the Israel Bible Center!

Dr. Eliyahu Lizorkin-Eyzenberg
President, Israel Bible Center
December 2017 – Kislev 5778

THE HEBREW TORAH

Don't Mess with Abraham!

Genesis 12:3 is a very well-known verse: "And I will bless those who bless you, and the one who curses you I will curse." That sounds clear, but a very important nuance is lost in translation.

The Hebrew verb meaning "to bless" is לְבָרֵךְ (*levarekh*), from the root ב-ר-ך (B-R-Kh). This root is connected to the concept of a "knee," and thus implies rendering service to someone (i.e., bending the knee). Hence, one possible meaning of the divine statement could be, "I will serve those who serve you!" To "serve" implies doing good for someone, bringing benefit to a recipient – thus "blessing."

In the second part of the verse God promised Abraham that "the one who curses you" מְקַלֶּלְךָ (*mekalelkha*) will in turn "be cursed" אָאֹר (*aor*). Notice that this promise (or threat!) uses two different words that are both translated as "to curse." The first of these, מְקַלֶּלְךָ (*mekalelkha*) comes from a root connected to the idea of "lightness" (as opposed to "heaviness"). The second word, אָאֹר (*aor*), derives from a completely different root that means something like "to utterly destroy."

Taking these Hebrew insights into consideration, an alternative possible translation of this famous verse might be as follows: "I will do good to those who do good to you, and the one who makes light of you I will utterly destroy."

The Blessing Meant for Jacob

Many believers struggle with understanding the Biblical figure of Jacob when they consider his life, at least privately. Their basic question may be expressed as, "How could a thief, a liar, and a coward be considered the father of God's people Israel?"

I believe that the blind, elderly Isaac had two different blessings in store for his sons. One was the blessing of the firstborn son, prepared for Esau, and the other was the blessing of Abraham, prepared for Jacob. The first was a general blessing of prosperity and power, but the second one had to do with the special calling of Abraham.

From this perspective, Jacob's place in the covenant was not based on his deception in tricking his father into thinking he was Esau. In fact, upon his return from Haran, Jacob sent reparations to Esau before meeting him. In doing so, he honestly acknowledged the sin of his youth and returned that which he had stolen (Gen. 32:1-21). Prior to meeting Esau, Jacob's encounter with the angel of the LORD enabled him to overcome his fears (Gen. 32:22-30).

In the end, the brothers' lives may have followed the plan of their originally intended blessings. Esau did acquire prosperity and power (Gen. 27:28-29), but Jacob gained the blessing of Abraham, a heritage of children and land (Gen. 28:1-5).

How could a blessing stolen from his dispossessed brother Esau establish Jacob's legitimacy as the patriarch of God's people? The answer is that it did not. The blessing of Abraham was always intended to pass to Jacob.

Was Tamar a Saint or a Sinner (or Both)?

Judah, one of Jacob's children, participated in a conspiracy to get rid of his half-brother Joseph by selling him as a slave. Given the short life expectancy of Egyptian slaves (usually twenty years or less), Joseph had escaped one death plot only to fall victim to an apparent slow, painful death in a foreign land.

Judah later fathered three sons, two of whom died after marrying Tamar (in sequence). Despite the custom of levirate marriage that obligated Judah to have his third son marry Tamar as well, year after year he refused. His love for his son overcame his sense of justice toward Tamar.

This continued until Tamar orchestrated a remarkable plot. Pretending to be a prostitute, she seduced Judah. Her unconventional but courageous plan actually worked. She became pregnant, and the identity of the child's father was also proven. At this point Judah repented, admitting his guilt and declaring Tamar more righteous than himself (Gen. 38:1-27).

From a certain perspective, this seemingly sordid event represented one of the greatest redemptive breakthroughs in the history of the world! The book of Ruth celebrates Perez, the child of Tamar and Judah, as a crucial part of God's redemptive plan – one of the ancestors of King David (Ruth 4:11-17). What is even more important is that the Gospels include Perez among the forefathers of Jesus (Yeshua) the Messiah, and the book of Revelation refers to Jesus as the Lion from the tribe of Judah! Tamar's unusual actions played a major role in this story.

A Match Made in Heaven

During an early interaction, God told Moses (Moshe) that He would send His angel to guide Israel through the wilderness. God also warned the people of Israel not to disobey His messenger, "for he will not pardon [their] transgression" (Exod. 23:21).

Moses approached God with a very bold request indeed; He asked instead for God to personally accompany Israel. In fact, Moses refused to move anywhere without God's own personal presence (Exod. 33:15). Why did Moses risk challenging God? Why did he think that the original arrangement would not work?

God granted Moses his request and even agreed to allow Moses to view His backside as He passed by. At the end of this incredible experience, hearing the words that describe God's fundamentally gracious and forgiving nature (Exod. 34:6), Moses disclosed his real reason: "…Because this is a stiff-necked people. Pardon our iniquity and our sin, and take us for Your own!" (Exod. 34:9).

In other words, Moses' argument went as follows: God should go with Israel and forgive them, precisely because they are a stiff-necked people! Since God had already warned that His messenger would not forgive Israel if they rebelled against him (Exod. 23:21), Moses knew that his only hope lay in persuading God Himself to journey with them. While being hidden in the cleft of the rock, Moses became aware that YHWH (unlike His messenger) would forgive "iniquity, transgression, and sin"

(Exod. 34:7). Moses understood that Israel's future rested solely in the God of Israel and that He would be their Emmanuel (God with us). Israel had sins, and YHWH had forgiveness – a true match made in heaven.

"First Let Me Bury My Father"

Jesus (Yeshua) made some statements that sound disturbing to readers. One of these was directed to a man who asked for some time before making the commitment of becoming a full disciple. He said he needed to bury his father first.

Jesus answered in a surprising way, "Allow the dead to bury their own dead; but as for you, go and proclaim everywhere the kingdom of God" (Luke 9:60). He explained, "No one, after putting his hand to the plow and looking back, is fit for the kingdom of God" (Luke 9:62). In other words, one cannot keep looking back and still plow straight. Similarly, the proclamation of the kingdom of God requires one's full and urgent commitment.

But how could Israel's Messiah possibly call upon His followers to disobey one of the Ten Commandments – honoring one's father (Exod. 20:12)? One plausible explanation has to do with the first-century Jewish practice of a secondary burial. The first part of burial consisted in placing the deceased in a cave for a prolonged period of time. After the complete decomposition of the body, only the bones would remain. At this point people trained in the relevant Jewish traditions would collect the bones and place them in an ossuary ("bone box"). The ossuary would then be deposited into its final resting place in another cave or tomb that housed many such boxes.

So Jesus did not require the man to neglect his father's burial. Rather, He simply suggested that professionals trained in dealing with corpses could themselves transfer the bones when the right time came. The man did not need to delay for a long time but could become a disciple right away if he really wanted to do so.

"Unless You Hate Your Father and Mother…"

There are certain texts in the Bible that make modern Christ-followers cringe. Among the most difficult of these is the statement of Jesus (Yeshua) about the need to hate one's own father and mother in order to be His true disciple (Luke 14:26). The key to resolving this difficulty lies hidden in the ancient meaning of the Hebrew word שָׂנֵא (sane), translated as "hate."

We read that God loved Jacob but "hated" Esau (Mal. 1:3). However, we can also see that in reality God blessed Esau greatly (Gen. 33:9), even warning the Israelites not to attack his descendants lest they risk the withdrawal of His protection from them (Deut. 2:4-6). In another place, Jacob is said to have "hated" his first wife Leah. Upon closer reading, however, it becomes clear that Jacob simply loved Rachel more than Leah (Gen. 29:30-31).

Furthermore, according to the Torah the God of Israel permits divorce based upon certain stringently defined circumstances that would make a marital relationship impossible to continue (Deut. 24:1-4). When our translation indicates that God "hates" divorce (Mal. 2:16), here too we must interpret it according to its original meaning in the ancient context. Israel's God regarded divorce and remarriage as "second-best" – not the ideal way to conduct human relationships.

All of these examples show that the idea of "hating" in Biblical Hebrew could include the notion of "loving less" or "preferring someone/something else."

So, then, did Jesus call upon people to stop honoring their parents? Most definitely not! The Messiah did, however, call His followers to a life of radical discipleship and overwhelming love for Him, such that even their very great love for their own parents would seem pale and weak by comparison.

"Unless Your Righteousness Surpasses..."

Jesus (Yeshua) said to His followers, "Unless your righteousness surpasses that of the scribes and Pharisees, you will not enter the kingdom of heaven" (Matt. 5:20). According to traditional interpretations, those Jesus referred to as "scribes and Pharisees" represented the holiest Jews. But was it really so?

First, some scribes were known for making alterations to the texts. In the book of Revelation, Jesus even issued a warning to future scribes, who would copy the text, to preserve the original words accurately: "If anyone adds to them… and if anyone takes away from the words of the book of this prophecy, God will take away his part from the tree of life" (Rev. 22:18-19). Even though people did not view scribes in the same negative light as tax collectors, for example, they may have seemed like a religious elite that did not actually have a high level of righteous living.

Second, at least some did not consider Pharisees to be counted among the most righteous of Jews. This view was most notably expressed by the Essenes, a contemporary Jewish sect whose writings were partly preserved in the Dead Sea Scrolls collection. The Essenes believed that the Pharisees had essentially "sold" Jerusalem to the Greeks and had conspired with God's enemies, compromising the holiness of the Temple. To emphasize their views, they referred to the Pharisees as "the seekers of smooth-things" (דורשי החלקות), as opposed to the preferred name for themselves – "the seekers of the paths [of God]" (דורשי ההלכות). In short, these Jews (Essenes) did not have a high estimation of Pharisaic righteousness (see Dead Sea Scroll text 4Q169).

In the light of these examples, we should conclude that Jesus' words should be taken literally – the level of righteousness of the scribes and Pharisees was indeed not enough to enter God's Kingdom. God requires much more!

What Did Jesus Teach about Divorce?

In the Gospel of Mark, Judean Pharisees came to Jesus (Yeshua) and asked Him whether it was lawful for a man to divorce a woman (Mark 10:1-12). In discussing this question, Jesus stated, "Whoever divorces his wife and marries another commits adultery against her, and if she divorces her husband and marries another, she commits adultery." This sounds like a complete denial of any legitimacy for divorce and remarriage at all, in any case.

However, the version of the story in the Gospel of Matthew clarifies the nature of the question they were discussing. No follower of the God of Israel at the time of Jesus would have thought it possible that the Word of God given through Moses had erred in permitting divorce (see Deut. 24:1-4; Exod. 21:10-11). Though different schools debated the circumstances that permitted divorce, none thought it forbidden in all cases. The fuller version of the story in the Gospel of Mathew helps to clarify this context. There we read the fuller question, "Can a man divorce a woman for any reason?" (Matt. 19:3-9).

A conservative Jewish approach understood "unfaithfulness," "abuse," or "abandonment" as the only valid grounds for divorce. Various more progressive Jewish interpreters argued that a man had the right to divorce his wife for any reason at all (see Babylonian Talmud, Gittin 90a). When Jesus was faced with this question, He rejected the idea taught by the Pharisees of the house or school of Hillel (divorce for any reason), siding instead with the Pharisees of the house of Shammai and the Essenes (divorce only in stringently defined situations).

Did Jesus Build "Fences" around the Torah?

An early Rabbinic Jewish text describes the functions of a Torah teacher in the following way: "The sages said three things…: Be very careful in judgment, raise up many disciples, and make a fence around the Torah" (Mishnah, Avot 1:1). The first two of these make sense to us even today without any difficulty. But what was meant by building a "fence" around the Torah?

The analogy of a physical fence is meant to communicate the notion of establishing a protective enclosure around God's commandments. A "fence" around the Torah is an extra layer of rules. In theory, one would first have to break the "fence" and then go further before actually falling into a transgression of the actual commandment of God.

In Matthew 5:27-28 we read, "You have heard that it was said, 'You shall not commit adultery;' but I say to you that everyone who looks at a woman with lust for her has already committed adultery with her in his heart." Here Jesus (Yeshua) quotes the original commandment ("Do not commit adultery!"), then adds, "But I say to you," and then states his "fence" ("Don't lust in your heart!").

Of course, Jesus was sometimes highly critical of Pharisaic "fences" around the Torah, arguing that they sabotaged the true deeper meaning of the Torah (see Mark 7:14-23). Yet we can see that He had a similar practice in terms of adding an extra layer of protection intended to guard the human heart against offending God. However, all of his "fences" (if we want to use that term) were rooted in the Torah itself, which also instructs people not to covet (i.e., desire wrongly) or hate one's fellow.

Did Jesus Declare All Foods Clean?

In Mark 7 we read about a sharp debate between Judean Pharisees and Jesus (Yeshua) over the fact that His Galilean disciples did not follow an important Pharisaic innovation. This innovation had to do with the perceived need to ensure that prior to consuming ritually clean, appropriate, and properly prepared food, a person must also wash their hands in order to avoid accidentally "profaning" (making common) something that was already holy. By the time the debate occurred, this Pharisaic innovation had already become "a tradition of the elders" and was treated respectfully as such by most Judeans (Mark 7:1-4).

Quoting Isaiah, Jesus accused the Pharisees of neglecting the commandments of the Torah itself, holding instead to the traditions of man (v. 8). Addressing the assembled crowd, Jesus stated, "There is nothing outside the man which can defile him if it goes into him; but the things which proceed out of the man are what defile the man" (v. 15). This statement may be understood as a summary of the regulations governing bodily discharges, as spelled out in Leviticus 15. By definition, bodily discharges come out of the body and do not enter into it. According to Jesus, this principle expresses a much deeper spiritual reality: namely, that evil comes out into the world from the human heart, from the inside out, rather than the other way around (vs. 20-23).

Some who rightly seek to reclaim the intensely Jewish character of Mark's Gospel have suggested that Mark 7:19 includes an editorial insertion made by Gentile Christians who misunderstood the Jewish context. In some translations, the end of that verse reads, "*Thus He declared* all foods clean." Certain analysts suggest that this entire line was added, thus distorting Mark's intention. Others argue that the words "Thus He declared," which are not in the Judeo-Greek text, have been mistakenly added by translators, who misunderstood the original language.

My own view is somewhat different: the controversial line actually completes Mark's very Jewish argument! Defending the original Torah against Pharisaic innovations, Jesus upholds a long-standing Jewish tradition, perhaps one practiced at his home in the Galilee. With the law of bodily discharges in mind, he declares that eating without washing one's hands cannot make an Israelite unclean, because in the Torah uncleanness actually comes out from inside! (Note that they were not discussing which animals to eat – a very different question. Lev. 11 describes how touching the meat of certain animals would indeed make a person temporarily "unclean.")

Did Jesus Know the Future?

On one occasion Jesus (Yeshua) instructed Peter (Shimon) and John (Yochanan) to prepare to celebrate the Passover. He said, "Enter a city, and then look for a man carrying a jar of water. Follow him, and ask the person in charge to offer hospitality. He will show you a large room." This is exactly what happened (Luke 22:7-13).

Flavius Josephus, a first-century Jewish historian, wrote a description of a hospitality network that may help us to understand this event. Speaking of the Essenes, a Jewish group roughly equal in size to the Pharisees, Josephus remarked: "They have no single specific city, but many of them dwell in every city; and if any of their sect come from other places, they give to them what they have… There is, in every city where they live, one appointed particularly to take care of strangers."[1] Josephus also confirmed that many of the Essenes did not marry, which we also know from other sources. Instead, the Essenes chose to wholly dedicate themselves to God.

So why did the disciples need to look for a man carrying a water jar? The answer may be amazingly simple. In early agricultural societies women usually drew and carried water (as shown, for example, in various Biblical stories). The sight of an adult man carrying a water jar would therefore suggest that he had no wife – and that he might well belong to the Essene community, which was renowned for its hospitality!

---

[1] Flavius Josephus, *The Wars of the Jews*, II.8.4.

Did Jesus know the future? Absolutely! He was familiar with the hospitality network of the Essene movement and used this knowledge to predict exactly what would happen if the disciples followed His instructions.

Was Mary Magdalene Ever a Prostitute?

Mary Magdalene (Miriam of Magdala) is definitely one of the best-known female characters of the New Testament writings. She has been popularized in dozens of films, stories, and even in the popular rock opera *Jesus Christ Superstar*. In almost all these popular presentations she is portrayed as a former prostitute who comes to Jesus in the spirit of true repentance. While the Gospels are known for their graciousness toward women and men with moral failings, this interpretation probably misrepresents the person called Mary Magdalene.

The name Mary is actually an English form of the traditional Hebrew name Miriam (or Mariam in Aramaic). The Gospels mention several women with this name, including Miriam or Mary the mother of Jesus (Yeshua); Mary of Bethany, the sister of Martha and Lazarus; Mary the mother of James (Jacob) and Joseph; and Mary the wife of Cleopas.

At the same time, we should note the appearance of two unnamed women who are expressly identified as sexual sinners: the woman who anointed Jesus' feet with costly perfume, and an alleged adulteress whom the Pharisees brought before Jesus to see if He would condemn her. (This second incident is not found in most ancient manuscripts.) It is possible that the portrayal of these anonymous women has influenced perception of Mary Magdalene.

In fact, the Gospels do not support the notion that Mary Magdalene was once a prostitute. They tell us her name and that she was "Magdalene" or "of Magdala," probably a reference to a place named for its tower (Hebrew *migdal*). Perhaps this sobriquet also gives readers a hint of the towering personality of Mary herself.

Luke 8:2 mentions in passing that seven demons had come out of Mary of Magdala. Some chauvinistic interpretations simply assumed that these demons must have indicated sexual immorality or addiction. However, the Gospels never speak of demons of a sexual nature being cast out (including in this case).

Moreover, the identification of Mary Magdalene as a repentant prostitute comes from medieval interpretations that combined her portrayal with that of several other women, at least one of whom was indeed a prostitute. But Mary (Miriam) was one of the most common Hebrew names at the time! Just because someone named Mary was a prostitute does not mean that Mary Magdalene was one as well. The long and the short of it is that there is simply no Scriptural basis to link these "sinful women" stories to Mary Magdalene.

Why Could Mary Not Touch Jesus?

One text that remains an enigma to most Christ-followers is the post-resurrection story in which Jesus (Yeshua) instructs Mary (Miriam) to avoid touching Him because He has "not yet ascended to the Father" (John 20:17).

But what are the facts of this case?

Mary attempts to verify that she has seen the resurrected Jesus (v. 16). He tells her that she cannot touch Him (v. 17). Shortly afterwards, when all the disciples have gathered together, Christ appears to them. Thomas is not with this group that sees Jesus (vs. 19-21). Later, when the other disciples report to him that they have seen Jesus alive, he responds with skepticism (v. 24). Eight days later, Jesus unexpectedly appears again and challenges Thomas to touch Him, placing his hands where the nails had pierced His body (vs. 26-27).

These facts beg the obvious question: Why did Jesus encourage Thomas to touch Him, yet deny Mary?

As a high priest Jesus would soon minister in the heavenly tabernacle on the Day of Atonement (Heb. 9:11). God had commanded Moses that priests must be purified before entering His presence. While "defilement" did not constitute a sin, it did disqualify one from service for a set period of time. One type of defilement for the Jewish high priest consisted in coming into any contact with death. Had this occurred, the priest would be disqualified for a time from public service to the Lord of Life (see Lev. 21:1-4). Thus, a most likely reason for Jesus' instructions to Mary concerned her contact with the tomb shortly prior to meeting the resurrected Jesus (v. 11). Another possibility is that Jesus was avoiding Mary's touch, because she may have been impure due to her monthly period (Lev. 15:19). His refusal may have been related to the high priestly purity that he was determined to preserve.

Why could Mary not touch Jesus? Because her Rabbi and Lord was soon to fulfill His priestly work.

The Lion of the Tribe of Judah

While reaching out to Samaritan Israelites, Jesus (Yeshua) did not hide His Judean perspective. He said, "You Samaritans worship what you do not know; we [Judeans] worship what we do know" (John 4:22a). The Samaritan community rejected the claims of David's family to the throne of Israel. Nonetheless, the Samaritan woman who heard these words seemed to accept the reasoning of the young prophet. When he said, "Salvation is from the Jews/Judeans" (John 4:22b), she undoubtedly understood this to mean, "Salvation comes from the tribe of Judah."

It is likely that Jesus had a text in mind when speaking with the Samaritan woman about salvation coming from the tribe of Judah. Before he died, the Hebrew patriarch Jacob blessed his sons. He reflected on the actions of each, including Judah, who was now mature and had repented of past misdeeds. Despite not being the firstborn, Judah received the following blessing: "You are a lion's cub, O Judah... The scepter shall not depart from Judah, nor the ruler's staff from between his feet, until he to whom it belongs comes; and he shall have the obedience of the nations" (Gen. 49:9-10). The book of Revelation would later explicitly equate Yeshua the Messiah (Jesus Christ) with the Lion from the tribe of Judah mentioned in Jacob's blessing (Rev. 5:5-6).

"If You Are the Messiah, Tell Us Clearly!"

"The Jewish authorities gathered around him, saying, 'How long will you keep us in suspense? If you are the Anointed One, tell us plainly.' Jesus answered, 'I did tell you, but you do not believe. The miracles I do in my Father's name speak for Me, but you do not believe because you are not My sheep'" (John 10:24-27). In this episode the Jerusalemite temple leadership challenged Yeshua to submit His candidacy for Messiahship to them. He refused, saying that His Father and His own deeds were enough to prove His Messiahship.

This text is most often read as an instance of Jesus' general lack of clarity on the topic. However, in my view the request should be read with a different emphasis than usual: not "How long will You keep us *in suspense*? If You are the Anointed One, tell us *plainly*"; but rather "How long will You keep *us* in suspense? If You are the Anointed One, tell *us* plainly."

The blind saw, the lame walked, lepers were cured, the deaf heard, and the dead came back to life (Matt. 11:2-5, Isa. 29:17-21). This should have made Yeshua's identity as Messiah self-evident. Israel's God had entrusted Him with authority; He therefore did not need the approval of a court of the Judean establishment (compare Matt. 26:62-64). Note that at this time many Judeans themselves strongly disliked their politico-religious leadership, which was often seen as corrupt, and thus might well have viewed Yeshua's response as appropriate.

How New Is the New Covenant?

The idea of the New Covenant as presented in the Gospels and the Pauline letters may sound like something completely new or innovative to modern Christ-followers. But is it really?

The ancient Hebrew prophet Jeremiah had declared that in the future the LORD would establish a New Covenant with the house of Israel and the house of Judah. This covenant, unlike the previous one, would be characterized by God's instruction (Torah) being written on the very hearts of the ancient people of God (Jer. 31:31-34).

So were there Jews in the first century who believed that they lived in the days of the New Covenant, even if they did not follow Jesus (Yeshua) as the Messiah? The answer to this interesting question is yes.

Thanks to several important archaeological discoveries, it has become clear that first-century followers of Jesus were not alone in laying claim to the idea of the New Covenant. For example, we read that some Jews called the members of their community "to observe the Sabbath according to its true meaning and the feasts and the day of the fast according to the utterances of them who entered into the New Covenant in the land of Damascus… To love each his brother as himself, and to strengthen the hand of the poor and the needy and the stranger" (Qumran Scrolls, Cairo Damascus Document 8:15-17).

The Jewish followers of Christ Jesus differed from this other Jewish group in that they were persuaded that the New Covenant had been inaugurated not near Damascus, but in the area of Jerusalem through the blood of Jesus (Matt. 26:26-29). How new was this New Covenant? The idea itself was a very old Jewish one.

Who Was the First Comforter?

On one occasion Jesus (Yeshua) made a curious promise to His disciples. He said, "I will ask the Father, and he will give you another Comforter" (John 14:16). This naturally raises the question of who the first Comforter was. And if that was Jesus Himself, then why did he use this curious phrasing?

Based on hymns found among the Dead Sea Scrolls, Professor Israel Knohl of the Hebrew University of Jerusalem – who is also a guest lecturer with us at the Israel Study Center – argued that one generation before Jesus a messianic leader arose who became known as the "Teacher of Righteousness." It may be possible to identify this person as Menachem the Essene, an advisor at the court of King Herod.

Menachem led a very dangerous life, secretly preparing for what eventually proved to be an unsuccessful revolt. His followers believed that he was the Messiah, but he was disgraced and killed by Roman soldiers during their revolt in 4 B.C.E. Later, according to Knohl, the Essenes reinterpreted his life as fulfilling the "suffering servant" texts in Isaiah.

The Hebrew word that lies behind the above-mentioned "Comforter" (in our translations from Jewish Greek) is in fact Menachem (מְנַחֵם), the same as the name of the Essene leader. The name itself means "Comforter."

When Jesus referred to the coming Holy Spirit as "another Comforter," was He identifying Himself as the first or true Menachem, Comforter of Israel? Perhaps He was specifically calling the Essene community to put its trust in Him. Unlike the failed revolt of Menachem the Essene, Jesus promised to lead a successful revolution against all the enemies of Israel – and even more, to overcome sin and death by His resurrection.

Who Said to Hold All Things in Common?

The book of Acts describes the first-century followers of Jesus Christ (Yeshua the Messiah) in a way that is unexpected for many modern believers. We read of what seems like a utopian society, whose members possessed all things in common, enabling the elimination of poverty and need (Acts 2:44-45). Their lifestyle represented the ultimate expression of the Jewish concept of *Ahavat Yisrael*, the love of Israel, as practiced among the Jewish followers of Jesus in the first century.

But how did this practice begin? On what basis did these believers conduct their communal lifestyle as followers of the Messiah? The Torah, though it emphasizes care for the poor and needy (Lev. 23:22), does not speak of sharing property in common. On the contrary, it seems to indicate a God-given right to private property (Exod. 20:17). Neither the prophets nor Yeshua taught that all the faithful must always abandon everything they ever owned. Yet these first-century believers still unapologetically adopted a communal lifestyle with shared property.

The best available reconstruction today links this group of Christ-followers with the Essene communities. According to the Jewish historian Josephus, the Essenes practiced just this kind of lifestyle. In describing them, he writes, "One cannot find a person among them who has more than another in terms of possessions… Those entering the community must yield up their funds to the order… The assets of each one have been mixed in together, as if they were brothers, to create one fund for all."[2]

If we imagine a community of believers in the Messiah Jesus who were rooted in the Essene movement, it makes perfect sense that they would have continued their longstanding traditional practice of pooling resources and sharing all in common.

---

[2] Flavius Josephus, *The Wars of the Jews*, II.8.3.

Did the Apostles Believe in the Trinity?

It is no secret that the Christian doctrine of the Trinity as such is not found in the Bible. Later Christians systematized this idea from various Biblical texts in an attempt to present one coherent and accurate teaching to unify all true believers. This traditional Christian doctrine holds that:

- The Father, the Son and the Holy Spirit are one God (not three Gods).
- The Father, the Son and the Holy Spirit are equal in power and glory (same in essence).
- The Father functionally is superior to the Son and the Holy Spirit (both Son and Spirit are obedient to the Father).

As we think through this important topic, we need to keep in mind a few things.

First, the original Christ-following movement maintained a very Jewish character, and as such was not very interested in doctrines *per se*. First-century Jews were not concerned so much with the details of correct beliefs, but rather the details of holy living.

Second, some Jews even prior to Jesus thought of the relation between God and his Word in nearly identical terms as does John's Gospel (John 1:1). Other pre-Jesus Jews, among many other intriguing understandings, believed in the notion of "the Son of Man" as an eternal heavenly being whom God would one day seat on the throne of His glory.

Third, while the apostles did not think of the Holy Spirit as simply God's power, devoid of any kind of personality (as in Jehovah Witnesses' theology), we nonetheless find embarrassingly little evidence for the divinity of the Holy Spirit in the New Testament writings.

I therefore conclude that if we were to present the apostles with the Christian doctrine of the Trinity in its traditional form, they would be deeply puzzled as to why such a systematization was necessary or considered essential. But then after being pressed for an answer, they would likely agree, albeit with some hesitation, that the basic ideas presented to them were indeed correct.

Did Shimon Peter Live as a Gentile?

The apostles Paul (Shaul) and Peter (Shimon) apparently argued about some matters of faith. Paul admonished Peter to live in accordance with the Gospel. As part of his argument, he claimed that Peter, though a Jew/Judean, "lived" like a member of the nations/Gentiles (Gal. 2:14). Had Peter abandoned the unique customs that all Jews were to observe?

Most commentators mistakenly believe that Paul was describing Peter's non-Jewish lifestyle. However, in that case Paul's argument would seem to make no sense. The very basis of the conflict between the two apostles suggests a different interpretation. After all, the conflict was about fellowship with Gentiles who had *not* gone through proselyte conversion. (A proselyte conversion from Gentile or pagan religions meant allegiance to Israel's God and also a commitment to follow the entire Law/Torah of Moses completely.)

In the first century many Gentiles accepted the Jewish Messiah (Christ) and worshiped Israel's God without obligating themselves to full Torah observance. They therefore remained members of the nations of the world; i.e., Gentiles. Jews had a problem fellowshipping with Gentiles not because they belonged to different nations, but because they followed different lifestyles – usually including immorality, idolatry, and other practices offensive to the God of Israel. Those Gentiles who followed Christ, however, were supposed to abandon these wrong deeds (even if they did not become proselytes/converts).

This background suggests a different way of understanding the argument between Paul and Peter. We should remember that Peter's apostolic commission led him to minister primarily to Jews/Judeans, while Paul focused on the nations/Gentiles. Paul also told Peter, "We who are Jews by birth and not Gentile 'sinners' know that a man is not justified by works of the Law" (Gal. 2:15-16a).

I think that Paul was not referring to Peter's lifestyle, but rather to his experience in Christ. Peter had witnessed how Israel's God poured out His Spirit on Gentile God-fearers (Acts 10). These Gentile God-fearers became recipients of the Holy Spirit of Israel's God – without becoming proselyte converts! So this phrase, "live like a Gentile," did not necessarily mean that Peter had abandoned his Jewish lifestyle. Perhaps Paul meant to imply instead that Peter was now alive in Christ *in exactly the same way* as Gentiles, by grace through faith and not simply because of obedience to the Law (Eph. 2:1-22).

Did Peter and Paul "live" like Gentiles? Absolutely! They were made "alive" in Christ in the same way as Gentiles!

Was the *Shema* Important to Paul?

In Deuteronomy 6:4, we read: "Hear, O Israel! The LORD is our God; the LORD is one." Known as the *Shema*, this has been the most important text for both ancient and modern Judaism.

For the apostle Paul (Shaul), the phrase "The LORD is our God" referred to Israel's covenantal bond with YHWH; while the phrase "The LORD is One" referred to the idea of the nations joining Israel in worship of YHWH. Strikingly, Paul was not alone in his thinking. We find good reason to affirm Paul's views as representative of a contemporaneous (and later) Jewish viewpoint. Let us consider several Jewish sources that place the apostle Paul firmly within the Jewish matrix of thought regarding this issue. (For an expended treatment consult *Paul and the Jewish Tradition: The Ideology of the Shema* by Mark Nanos.)

A commentary on the book of Deuteronomy written in the third century stated:

"'The LORD, our God,' over us [the children of Israel]; 'the LORD is one,' over all the creatures of the world. 'The LORD, our God,' in this world; 'the LORD is one,' in the world to come. As it is said, 'The LORD will be king over all the earth. In that day will the LORD be one and His name one'" (Sifre on Deut. 6:4).

A commentary on Deuteronomy written in the eleventh century stated:

"The LORD who is our God now, but not [yet] the God of the [other] nations is destined to be the One LORD, as it is said… 'And the LORD shall be king over all the earth; on that day shall the LORD be One and His name One'" (Rashi on Deut. 6:4).

The big difference between the Jews who authored the above-mentioned writings and the apostle Paul comes down to this: Paul was convinced that the time of the ingathering of the nations (described by the prophets) had already arrived, while the others were not.

We see the centrality of the *Shema* in Paul's letters in many instances. Below I point out just a few representative examples.

Paul acknowledged that other people groups love and worship their own gods. Yet he wrote that the reality remains: "There is but one God":

"Therefore, concerning the eating of things sacrificed to idols, we know that there is no such thing as an idol in the world, and that there is no God but one. For even if there are beings who are called gods, whether in heaven or on earth, as indeed there are many gods and many lords, yet for us there is but one God, the Father, from whom are all things and for whom we exist, and one Lord, Jesus Christ, by whom are all things and through whom we exist" (1 Cor. 8:4-6).

In a letter written from prison, Paul calls Christ-followers to covenantal unity based on the oneness of God:

"Therefore I, the prisoner of the Lord, implore you to walk in a manner worthy of the calling with which you have been called… There is one body and one Spirit, just as also you were called in one hope of your calling; one Lord, one faith, one baptism, one God and Father of all who is over all and through all and in all" (Eph. 4: 1-5).

In his letter to the Romans, Paul argued in the form of a rhetorical question that the God of Israel is also the God of the nations (Gentiles):

"Or is God the God of Jews only? Is He not the God of Gentiles also? Yes, of Gentiles also!" (Rom. 3:29).

Was the Shema important to Paul? Not just important – it held a central place in his theology!

Paul's Forgotten Rule

When asked, almost no one in the Christian world can answer this simple question: What one very important rule did the apostle Paul (Shaul) establish in all his congregations? Here is the answer from his own writings: "Each one should retain the place in life that the Lord assigned to him and to which God has called him. This is the rule I lay down in all the congregations. Was a man already circumcised when he was called? He should not become uncircumcised. Was a man uncircumcised when he was called? He should not be circumcised" (1 Cor. 7:17-18).

When people "converted" in ancient times, they were not converting from one religion to another in a modern sense but rather from one people group to another. Members of both Israel and the nations were sometimes willing to completely cut ties with their communities and switch their communal alliances. Some Jews went through surgery that hid the signs of circumcision, while some non-Jews adopted Jewish ancestral ways of life (including circumcision, which came to stand for the whole process of becoming a proselyte).

The great apostle Paul believed that Israel and the nations, while retaining their distinct identities, should worship God jointly. In his view of a New Covenant community, there should be no discrimination between Jews and Gentiles, but a functional distinction between the two groups should also continue to exist.

Paul's reasoning was simple. If Gentile Christ-followers became Jews, then the God they worshipped would be too small. He would be the God of the Jews only. If, however, Gentile Christ-followers, as representatives of the nations of the world, would worship Israel's God alongside the Jews, then the grandeur of this one God would become evident to all (Rom. 3:28-30).

Was Paul Right about Women?

In 1 Cor. 14:34 the apostle Paul (Shaul) wrote: "The women should keep silent in the assemblies. For they are not permitted to speak, but should be in submission, as the Law also says." This statement contains several major problems we must deal with.

First, nowhere does the Torah forbid women to speak in public gatherings. Paul, being a well-educated Jew, certainly would have known this. In fact, a law at the time did exist that forbade women to speak, vote, or exercise authority over men by holding public office. Yet it was not a Jewish but rather a Roman law. Thus, these words sound far more credible if referring to that (non-Jewish) law.

Second, on numerous occasions throughout his travels and letters the apostle Paul affirmed the ministry of women (Rom. 16:3-4; 1 Cor. 16:19; cf. Acts 16:11-40; 18:26). The centrality of the *Shema* – the oneness of Israel's God – informed Paul's theology when he wrote that Christ-following assemblies should have no tolerance for segregation or discrimination:

"There is neither Jew nor Greek, there is neither slave nor free man, there is neither male nor female; for you are all one in Christ Jesus" (Gal. 3:28).

In 1 Cor. 11:5, he wrote that a woman's head must be covered while she engages in speaking in tongues or prophesying in a public assembly. He did not question, therefore, *if* a woman could speak and teach in the assembly, but rather *how* it should be done in a way that would be right before God, angels, and the people of Corinth.

Whenever we read Paul's letters, we need to keep in mind that 1 Corinthians did not mark the beginning of this correspondence. In fact, Paul wrote at least one other letter to the Corinthians prior to this letter (see 1 Cor. 5:9), and the Corinthian leadership had also written to him previously (see 1 Cor. 7:1).

One possible reading of the verse in question maintains that 1 Cor. 14:34-35 appears as a quotation from a letter that the Corinthian male leadership had addressed to Paul. Speculatively, they had proposed a way of bringing order to the disruptive practice in which some women in the congregation were speaking in tongues and prophesying. Paul, however, disagreed.

If we then view this text as a quotation, the challenge in 1 Cor. 14:36 that Paul brings to the male leadership makes perfect sense:

"Or was it from you that the word of God first went forth?! Or has it come to you only?!"

Paul instructed the all-male leadership of the Corinthian congregation not to forbid women from speaking in tongues. He also encouraged them to prophecy, just as the women among them already were doing:

"Therefore, my brethren, desire earnestly to prophesy, and do not forbid to speak in tongues. But all things must be done properly and in an orderly manner" (1 Cor. 14:39-40).

Paul's solution, therefore, did not exclude half of the congregation from exercising the gifts of the Spirit, but rather sought to make sure that they did so in a respectful, proper, and orderly fashion.

Was Paul right about women? Absolutely! It may be that his Corinthian opponents were not.

Did Paul Instruct Timothy to Eat Unclean Food?

The apostle Paul (Shaul) wrote that he had instituted the following rule in all congregations that he established:

"Was any man called circumcised? He is not to become uncircumcised. Has anyone been called in uncircumcision? He is not to be circumcised" (1 Cor. 7:17-19).

Paul demonstrated this principle, on the one hand, by not compelling Titus (a Greek) to be circumcised (Gal. 2:3). Then on the other hand, he supported circumcising Timothy because he was actually Jewish (the son of a Jewish mother and a Greek father). Knowing that his Jewish co-worker Timothy had not been circumcised, Paul apparently anticipated that his own consistency regarding circumcision could be rightly challenged by the local Jewish community (Acts 16:3).

Sometime later Paul wrote to Timothy:

"Some will fall away from the faith… forbidding marriage, abstaining from foods which God has created to be gratefully shared in by those who believe and know the truth. For everything created by God is good, and nothing is to be rejected if it is received with gratitude, for it is sanctified by means of the word of God and prayer" (1 Tim. 4:1-4).

Based on the assumption that Paul was referring to the unclean meats in the Torah, one traditional interpretation implies that he was instructing Timothy to completely oppose the Torah's division of animals into "clean" and "unclean." Such a reading, however, presents problems for two reasons:

First, such an interpretation ignores the universally upheld Jewish idea that the entire creation is good, because God declared it so (see Gen. 1:25). Second, just because God's creation is good, we cannot assume that all of it is therefore suitable as food for the Israelites (see Lev. 11:13). In fact, Paul specifically stated that anything can be eaten only when two specific conditions are met: God has sanctified it by His Word, and the worshiper has sanctified it by his/her prayer (1 Tim. 4:4).

Paul therefore instructed Timothy to remember, especially after his circumcision, that he must honor the God of Israel in every detail of his life as a Christ-following Jew, including the way he ate.

Did Paul instruct Timothy to eat unclean food? No, in fact he told him the exact opposite!

Why Was Paul Against Circumcision?

Circumcision has been and remains one of the most important markers of Jewish identity. It testifies both to Israel's trust in God regarding its future and to God's promise justifying that trust.

The question, therefore, is indeed a significant one: Why did the apostle Paul oppose circumcision for Gentiles? After all, he expressed this opposition while professing to be a true Pharisee! (Acts 23:6) Yet this occurred after his encounter with the risen Jewish Christ.

The answer is not as complicated as it may first appear.

The apostle Paul, as most Jews during his lifetime, used the word "circumcision" as a code word for Jewish identity (Col. 4:11). While he thought that being a Judean was an advantage in many ways (Rom. 3:1-2), he still adamantly opposed Gentile proselyte conversion to Judaism. His reasoning resulted from a belief that something significant had happened – Gentiles had also become recipients of the gift of the Holy Spirit. Those receiving this gift from God were not converts to Judaism, but rather Gentile God-fearers not attempting to become Jews (Eph. 3:6; Acts 15:7-8).

If all Gentile Christ-followers were to go through the proselyte conversion and become Jews in every way, it would sabotage God's cosmic plan of revealing himself to the world. Paul's Pharisaic idea was simple: Judeans should stay Judeans, and members of other nations should remain part of those nations.

And both must unite in worship of the one true God (1 Cor. 7:17-20).

Why was Paul against circumcision? Actually, he supported it as a Jewish practice. But this true Jew also held a strong conviction that the glory of Israel's God had to become known to the entire world! His God could not be the God of the Jews only; He is much greater than that (Rom. 3:29).

The Law of Moses and the Grace of God

"The new is in the old concealed; the old is in the new revealed," said Augustine. In contrast to the general tendency among many Christian believers, this quotation does not contrapose two parts of the Holy Bible. Rather, Augustine interconnects the "old" and the "new."

The majority of Bible translations have statements such as, "For the Law came through Moses, *but* grace and truth came through Jesus Christ" (John 1:17). Such readings do indicate a clear opposition. Even with a more accurate translation – "For the law was given through Moses; grace and truth were realized through Jesus Christ" – many readers automatically assume the same opposition.

The translation can be improved further. The Greek word (νόμος) often translated as "law" would be better as "Torah" (i.e., the Pentateuch), because this was the primary meaning of the word as used by Jews in the first century. The terms "grace" and "truth" are far less problematic, but the English words do not fully reflect the force of the spoken Hebrew that lies "behind" the written Greek. Therefore, we should read John 1:17 as follows: "The Torah came through Moses, and unfailing love [חָסָד] and truthfulness [אֱמֶת] came through Jesus Christ [or Yeshua the Messiah]" (my translation).

The grace and truth of God can be clearly seen in the Torah of Moses, while the Jewish Christ displays grace and truth to their utmost degree. The opposite of law was never grace, but rather lawlessness. The opposite of grace was never law, but rather disgrace.

The Gospel in the Hebrew Bible

One of the most important words found in the New Testament writings is εὐαγγέλιον (*euangelion*). Most translate this Greek word as "the Gospel." A literal translation, however, would be simply "news of good" or "good news."

When the armies of Israel faced those who sought to conquer their land and enslave their people, messengers stood ready to carry back home any news at all. In the case of defeat – a warning to run and hide; in the case of victory – encouragement to celebrate and rejoice!

We read in Isaiah 52:7:

מַה נָּאווּ עַל הֶהָרִים רַגְלֵי מְבַשֵּׂר, מַשְׁמִיעַ שָׁלוֹם מְבַשֵּׂר טוֹב... אֹמֵר לְצִיּוֹן, מָלַךְ אֱלֹהָיִךְ.

"How pleasant on the mountains are the feet of him who proclaims the good news of peace… and says to Zion, 'Your God reigns!'"

Such good news may be set in a military context, expressed in terms of Israel's God defeating His enemies. The announcement of God's victory provides a basic reason for Zion to rejoice. The apostle Paul, when describing the spectacular effect of the death, burial, and resurrection of Jesus (Yeshua), also defined *euangelion* in terms of the war-like defeat of the powers of darkness:

"When He had disarmed the rulers and authorities, He made a public parade of them [defeated], having triumphed over them by Himself" (Col. 2:15).

Even when referring to spiritual warfare, the Gospel still finds its roots in the texts of the Hebrew Bible. The victory of the Jewish Christ constituted the definitive victory of Israel's God over all His enemies, foreign and domestic. The resurrection of the crucified Christ means that Israel's God still reigns and that the powers of evil have already suffered their catastrophic defeat.

Torah and the Apostle Paul

The event and rituals associated with becoming a Bar Mitzvah (literally "son of [the] commandment") play an important role in the modern Jewish life cycle. While the ceremony as practiced today has medieval origins, some of its fundamental concepts trace back to the first century or earlier.

At the age of thirteen, boys participate for the first time in the public Torah reading as adults – leading the synagogue in congregational worship. The father, however, plays an interesting role within this wonderful ceremony.

He pronounces a short blessing: בָּרוּךְ שֶׁפְּטָרַנִי מֵעׇנֶשׁ הַלָּזֶה (*barukh shepetarani meonesh halazeh*). Translated, it means something like this: "Blessed is He who has released me from [the responsibility] of punishment over this one."

Until the time of becoming a Bar Mitzvah, the father has responsibility over his son. He is to offer him close guidance until such time as he will be able to engage with the Torah on his own. The idea here is not that the thirteen-year-old son is no longer in need of parental guidance. It does not mean that the boy is now permitted to desist from honoring his father or should no longer obey him. But it means that from this point on he is now considered competent to engage with Torah in his own right.

It is possible that the apostle Paul, who was steeped in Pharisaic Judaism of the first century, had a similar idea. He understood, together with some other Jews of his time, that the coming of the Jewish Christ brought about some kind of transfer of responsibility.

In one of his letters to the Gentile followers of the Jewish Christ, the apostle Paul wrote about his countrymen's experience with the Torah:

"Before the coming of the faith, we were closely guarded by the Torah (ὑπὸ νόμον ἐφρουρούμεθα συγκλειόμενοι), until the faith that was to come would be revealed. The Torah was our guardian (ὁ νόμος παιδαγωγος) until Christ came, that we might be justified by faith. Now that the faith has come, we are no longer under a guardian" (Gal. 3:23-25).

Later in the same letter, he states that Gentiles are now in the same position as Christ-following Jews. They too must be guided not only by the Torah (no matter how wonderful and good it is), but also through direct interaction with the Holy Spirit sent by Israel's God at the request of King Jesus (see John 14:26). In Galatians 5:18 he writes:

"But if you are led by the Spirit, you are not under the Torah."

Paul believed that a new age had dawned with the coming of the Messiah. This meant that the Christ-following Jews were no longer guided by the Torah (like a tutor), but also through personal faith in Christ Jesus. However, just as in the case of the father and the Torah, the believers were not to disregard the Torah simply because they were now interacting directly with someone who was even greater – Christ Jesus through God's Holy Spirit!

Is There One Law for Everyone?

Many modern Christ-followers wonder whether the Law of Moses (Torah) applies equally to everyone. In a brilliant argument in one of his letters, Paul (Shaul) wrote that believers from the nations become part of the commonwealth of Israel, and because of their connection with the Jewish Messiah (Christ) receive the same rights and privileges as the kingdom's original citizens (Eph. 2:11-22). Does the Torah of Israel then apply to Gentile Christ-followers also?

The answer is both yes and no. On the one hand, the Torah clearly has some applicability to everyone. The first-century council of leaders in Jerusalem highlighted only four categories of behavior forbidden to Gentile believers (Acts 15:19-21). This suggests that other important principles from the Torah were already familiar to these Christ-followers. Perhaps seven to ten percent of the entire population of the Roman empire was Jewish. Some Gentiles in the Roman world participated in Jewish synagogues, which were community centers that could have a shared public use.

On the other hand, the Torah was never meant to apply in the same way to everyone. It contains many laws and regulations applicable only to specific groups of people. For example, there are laws that are only applicable to Levites, others that are prescribed specifically for priests or high-priests, still others that pertain only to men or women, and yet others given only to sojourners or temporary residents in Israel.

So is there really one law for everyone? In some very important ways, certainly yes! But is the whole Torah applicable to everybody in the same way? Just as clearly not.

Gentile Christians and the Jewish Torah

Imagine being present at the special assembly convened by James (Yaakov) in Jerusalem in the first century. The account of Luke describes an impressive group of Judean, Galilean, and Diaspora-based elders and apostles who follow Jesus (Yeshua) as Israel's Messiah (Acts 15:6).

The assembly met to consider a crucial question. Should Gentiles who believe in the Messiah (Christ) join the Jewish people as "Jews in every way," or should they instead remain part of "the nations of the world"? Could one simply ally with the broader Jewish coalition, worshiping the God of Israel alongside native Jews, or was more required?

Two opposing opinions were represented at the council. Both views required some level of Torah observance (i.e., obeying certain laws given by God). The first option, commonly known as "proselyte conversion," required a long and complex process of "Judaizing" – learning and adopting the ancestral customs of the Jewish or Judean people. The second option was easier, allowing Gentiles to keep their non-Jewish identity while worshipping the God of Israel. The Pharisee Paul (Shaul) strongly believed that the second option was the right path to follow (1 Cor. 7:17-20).

In the Roman world Gentile Christians faced significant difficulties at this time. By far the greatest of these was that Roman life required honoring pagan deities as a matter of daily life. In some cases Gentile Christ-followers could be excluded from participation in the local economy and accused of treachery against their fellow Roman citizens (see Rev. 13:17).

Based on what we know of the history of the time, Gentile believers would have held the stories of the Torah in high regard and maintained a good relationship with the Jewish community. They regularly participated in celebrating the festivals of Israel as a matter of course, worshipping the God of Israel and following the Jewish Christ.

The council in Jerusalem did not prescribe that these Gentile Christ-followers become Jews, but did insist that they avoid four things: food sacrificed to idols, (eating) blood, the meat of strangled animals, and sexual immorality (Acts 15:22-29). These categories of behavior had also been forbidden to sojourners or temporary residents in Israel (Lev. 17-18, 20).

While keeping their own national identities, Gentile Christians in the Roman world were thus instructed to observe part of the Jewish Torah. By extension, the same principles are applicable to all subsequent generations of Christians around the world.

Are Christians Now Jews?

It happens quite often that someone comes up to me and says, "Brother, where you go wrong is in distinguishing Jews and Gentiles, even though both are in Christ! Now there is neither Jew nor Gentile. Now we are all the same in Christ!"

Usually such people have in mind a passage like Galatians 3:27-29, where we read: "For all of you who were baptized into Christ have clothed yourselves with Christ. There is neither Jew nor Greek, there is neither slave nor free man, there is neither male nor female; for you are all one in Christ Jesus. And if you belong to Christ, then you are Abraham's descendants, heirs according to promise."

Now today words like "baptized" and "Christ" sound exclusively Christian. But in the time of the apostle Paul (Shaul), that was clearly not the case. In fact, in the first century these terms sounded exclusively Jewish!

When someone who was a Greek (i.e., Hellenistic pagan) underwent the Jewish ritual of immersion in water (traditionally called the *mikveh*) in the name of the Jewish Christ, in so doing he or she professed faith in Israel's God. According to the followers of Jesus (Yeshua), something very important happened at this time. Such a Hellenistic man or woman in some real way became a child of Abraham and co-heir, together with Jews, of the promises of Israel's God!

The distinction between Jews and Greeks/Gentiles was not abolished, just as the distinction between men and women was also not abolished. Instead, through fellowship in Christ Jesus (Messiah Yeshua) any discrimination between them was to vanish. Thus Jews and Gentiles were still distinct in their identities, but one was not to be preferred over the other. Similarly, in the kingdom of God men should not be preferred over women.

So are all Christ-followers now Jews? No, but they are part of the commonwealth of Israel – as members of the nations of the world, Gentiles can worship Israel's God through the Jewish Christ (Eph. 2:12). These Gentile believers are God's people along with the Jews, and heirs to promises of God together with them.

Why Don't (All) Jews Believe in Jesus?

Most modern Christ-followers mistakenly think that the New Testament states that the Jewish people rejected Jesus (Yeshua). But is this reading accurate?

The main proof text for the idea that "the Jews rejected Christ" comes from a traditional misreading of the Gospel of John. In a translation from the original Koine Judeo-Greek, we read, "He came unto His own, but His own received Him not" (John 1:11). The standard Christian interpretation of this verse equates "His own" with first-century people belonging to the Jewish religion. This view suffers from two fundamental errors.

First, the traditional interpretation ignores the grammar of the original. The first "own" is neuter (τὰ ἴδια), but the second "own" is masculine (οἱ ἴδιοι). This indicates that at least the first "His own" cannot possibly refer to the Jews – it must be talking about something else!

The second mistake relates to the fact that the first-century word traditionally translated as "Jews" (Ἰουδαῖοι) did not mean "people of the Jewish religion" as it does today. The primary meaning of this word in John's Gospel is "Judeans," or even "the leaders of the Judean region."

Paul wrote in 2 Cor. 3 about a "veil" covering the heart of some people of Israel (reminiscent of the veil that once covered Moses' face), and in Rom. 11 he used similar language to point out that this situation had brought about spiritual benefit for other nations. Yet nowhere in the Bible can we find the claim that "the Jews rejected Jesus."

The question that bothered the apostle Paul was actually: Why don't *all* Jews believe in Jesus (rather than only some)? He translates this concern into a crucial question, "Did God reject His people?" A very clear answer follows, "Absolutely not! .... For at the present time there is a remnant, chosen by grace" (Rom. 11:1, 5).

Luther, Hitler, and the Jews

From ancient times Christianity has struggled greatly with the so-called Jewish question. Only seventy to eighty years ago a Christian nation – albeit one ruled by deeply pagan, anti-Christian leadership – sought to eliminate Jews from the face of the earth completely.

How did things get so bad? This is certainly a legitimate question. Though many factors played a role, we can identify at least one of the most important reasons: a particular type of anti-Judaic Christian theology. Early Christianity imported an anti-Jewish bias from pre-Christian Greco-Roman authors and then nurtured this prejudice for centuries.

In the sixteenth century the famous German reformer Martin Luther gave a significant boost to this long-lived anti-Jewish element in Christian theology. In one of his later works, written when he felt angry at German Jews for various reasons, Luther ranted:

> What shall we Christians do with this rejected and condemned people, the Jews? ...First, set fire to their synagogues or shuls, and bury and cover with dirt whatever will not burn... Second, I advise that their houses also be razed and destroyed... Third, I advise that all their prayer books and Talmudic writings, in which such idolatry, lies, cursing, and blasphemy are taught, be taken from them. Fourth, I advise that their rabbis be forbidden to teach henceforth on pain of loss of life and limb... Fifth, I

>advise that safe conduct on the highways be abolished completely for the Jews…[3]

In twentieth-century Europe Adolf Hitler and those close to him believed that Christianity was a "bastard child" of Judaism. Hitler's theologians used this text by Martin Luther to convince many Protestant leaders and congregants to turn a blind eye to his anti-Jewish policies. In many cases German Protestants enthusiastically supported creating Jewish ghettos and work camps.

What must we do today in light of this tragic history? Jewish and Gentile believers must stand together to prevent any other holocausts from happening in our world, among Jews or any other people.

---

[3] Martin Luther, *On the Jews and Their Lies* (1543).

Will the Temple Be Rebuilt?

The prospect of rebuilding the temple in Jerusalem continues to captivate the hearts and minds of millions of Jews and Christians around the world. When will it be rebuilt? Will there still be animal sacrifices? What would happen next? Sincere Christians also ask questions like: How will the Temple service function and apply, given the sacrifice Jesus already offered on the cross?

People today have many opinions about the possibility of such a building project. The "New Testament" (writings about the New Covenant, or *Ha-Brit Ha-Chadashah* in Hebrew) affirms great respect for God's Temple in Jerusalem. At the same time, its authors posit that the Jewish Christ (Messiah) and those who believe in Him are themselves the ultimate temple of God (1 Pet. 2:5). One of the clearest examples of this connection is the incarnation of Jesus as described in John's Gospel, in terms of God "tabernacling among us" (John 1:14).

Another passage establishes a direct connection with the eschatological temple described by Ezekiel. At the priestly water-pouring ceremony during the Feast of Tabernacles, Jesus declared, "He that believes in me, as the Scripture has said, out of his belly will flow rivers of living water" (John 7:38). The Scripture to which Jesus was referring describes a river that makes the desert green and resurrects all dead things. That river flows out of the interior of the temple that Ezekiel saw (Ezek. 47:1-9).

So will the temple be rebuilt? Perhaps, but we must always remember that the ultimate temple is comprised of the person of the Jewish Christ and the lives of His Jewish and Gentile followers.

Revelation: The Apocalypse or Unveiling

What Is the "Lord's Day"?

The book of Revelation is a Jewish letter written in the first century from an anti-Roman perspective. In this vision the Jewish Christ or Messiah acts as the High Priest of the Heavenly Temple, walking amidst seven golden lampstands (Rev. 1:10-13). He speaks a message of warning and encouragement to seven real assemblies, who were struggling to be loyal to Israel's God in following the Jewish Christ as residents of an unapologetically pagan Roman empire.

John's vision is characteristic of the Jewish apocalyptic tradition, which includes many similar accounts. He tells us about finding himself "in the spirit on the Lord's day" (Rev. 1:10). Many readers now wonder whether John had in mind the seventh day (the Israelite Sabbath) or the first day of the week (Sunday, and the day of Jesus' resurrection). This can even connect to modern controversies about rest and worship days.

Both Sabbath and Sunday interpretations are possible, but both are also problematic for various reasons. Neither the Sabbath day nor Sunday was ever called "the Lord's day" prior to this point. Now, perhaps John invented a new terminology in his letter. After all, there is a first time for everything, right? However, in this case another possibility exists that seems to make more sense.

The Hebrew prophets spoke often of "the day of the LORD" (see, for example, Isa. 2:12-22). According to Isaiah, this is the day when justice will finally prevail, as the God of Israel judges His enemies and rewards His faithful children with peace and prosperity. When Revelation speaks of "the Lord's day," it is most probably referring to this same "day of the LORD" – an interpretation that makes sense linguistically and fits very well with the context in the rest of John's account.

So did the first-century Jew who wrote Revelation mean Saturday or Sunday when he wrote of the Lord's day? Almost certainly neither. He intended us to understand the LORD's day of judgment and justice foretold centuries earlier by the Hebrew prophets!

What Was the Throne of Satan?

When interpreting the book of Revelation, we should take account of its thoroughly Jewish and anti-Roman nature. In Revelation 2:12-13 we read the following address to the followers of Jesus (Yeshua) in the city of Pergamum: "These are the words of him who has the sharp, double-edged sword. I know where you dwell, where Satan's throne is."

Besides a temple dedicated to the emperor and even one devoted to the goddess Roma, the city of Pergamum had the honor of hosting and maintaining a temple to Zeus, father of the gods and ruler of Olympus. In addition, the largest healing center in the Middle East was also located in Pergamum – the Asclepeion or healing temple dedicated to Asclepius, the son of Zeus. Very likely the reference to the "throne of Satan" in Revelation refers to one of these enormous pagan structures, or to all of them collectively.

The same passage uses the image of a double-edged sword, which is also highly symbolic. Christ-followers in the Roman empire needed to know that even in a deeply pagan city like Pergamum, ultimate authority and power belonged not to Zeus and Asclepius but rather to the God of Israel and His son, the Jewish Christ.

666 or 616?

Gematria is a well-known Jewish interpretive method that assigns the numerical values of Hebrew letters to words, phrases, or even sentences. By adding the numbers together, this technique seeks to determine a deeper meaning. Sometimes the connections may be farfetched, but other times they are clear and relevant.

In Matthew's genealogy, which shows that Jesus (Yeshua) was a descendant of King David, we read, "Thus there were fourteen generations in all from Abraham to David, fourteen from David to the exile to Babylon, and fourteen from the exile to the Messiah" (Matt. 1:17).

Now, the numerical value of the Hebrew characters forming the name David (דוד), the great king of Israel, is itself 14. Here is how it works: ד (4) + ו (6) + ד (4) = 14. Thus Matthew interweaves gematria and genealogy to tie Jesus to David three times. His point is that Jesus is the ultimate son of David; in other words, the Messiah.

In the book of Revelation we read, "Here is wisdom. Let him who has understanding calculate the number of the beast, for the number is that of a man; and his number is six hundred and sixty-six" (Rev. 13:18). The author clearly says that the number of the beast can be calculated, which is a clear hint to do exactly that. Although this figure of the "beast" is almost certainly not limited to the first century only, we can learn a great deal by considering the historical context at the time when the book of Revelation was written. The Emperor Nero was a bloodthirsty persecutor of early Christ-followers. It just so happens that his name written Hebrew (נרון קסר) has a numerical value of 666.

Christian tradition says that both Peter (Shimon) and Paul (Shaul) were martyred during Nero's reign. It is likely that Nero came to symbolize all such government-sponsored persecutions (even future ones). This would help explain the code in Revelation, and why the "beast" has the number 666.

This approach also helps explain why some early manuscripts of the book of Revelation have 616 instead of 666 as the number of the beast. The above calculation is based on a Hebrew spelling of the Greek version of Nero's name, which would have been used in the eastern Roman empire. However, if one instead uses the Latin version of his name when writing in Hebrew (נרו קסר), then the calculation yields 616 – while still referring to the same Nero and using the same technique of gematria.

What Was the Mark of the Beast?

The book of Revelation includes a text describing the arrival of an evil "beast," the enemy of God's people. At this time, we read, Christ-followers will be excluded from participating in the local economy unless they agree to place the mark of the beast upon their head and hand (Rev. 13:16-18).

To understand the original meaning of this "mark of the beast," we need to know some Biblical background. The central Jewish text that is recited twice daily declares, "Hear, O Israel! The LORD is our God, the LORD is one." The next part is less famous but also essential, "And you shall bind them [God's commandments] as a sign on your hand, and they shall be on your forehead" (Deut. 6:4-8).

If the book of Revelation is read with awareness of the first-century Jewish context, the meaning of many seemingly odd phrases becomes evident. To grasp this passage, we need not wonder whether one day all people will undergo a medical procedure in which a chip will be inserted under human skin. Instead we can understand the mark of the beast as a clear, outwardly expressed opposition to the commandment to worship the God of Israel alone.

In the first century many Christ-followers and their children wondered deeply about the nature and limits of this commandment in Deuteronomy. They considered whether it was possible to publicly honor some Roman deities while privately maintaining their worship of Israel's God through the Jewish Christ. If that were possible, it could ensure their economic survival and prosperity under the watchful eye of the Roman authorities. However, the book of Revelation advocates an unapologetically Israelite, anti-Roman position – only worship of the one true God of Israel is permitted.

What Is Armageddon?

The letter or book of Revelation speaks about a bowl of God's wrath that will one day be poured out upon the enemies gathered to fight God's people in the place called Armageddon. The verse explicitly states that this is the Hebrew name of the place, though spelled out in the letter in Greek (Rev. 16:16).

Megiddon (or Megiddo, Magiddon) was once a Canaanite city southeast of Mount Carmel (near modern-day Haifa). It was eventually conquered by Joshua and assigned as a territory of the tribe of Manasseh (see Josh. 12:21, 17:11; Zech. 12:11). The meaning of the place name *Megiddon* is uncertain, but the most likely explanation is that it comes from the Hebrew root ג-ד-ד (G-D-D or *gadad*), which carries the basic meaning of "cutting" or "invading."

The valley of Megiddon has been the site of numerous military conflicts throughout history. Solomon fortified the city and stationed cavalry stood there, ready to be dispatched to defend Israel's northern borders from invaders at any time (1 Kgs. 9:15-19). Ancient Israel represented a passageway connecting the trade routes running between Europe, Africa, and Asia. Therefore, whoever controlled that region would have a powerful economic position. (One modern Hebrew word for a "road" comes from the root meaning "to conquer.")

The name *Armageddon* is a Greek combination of two Hebrew words: הַר (*har*, "mountain, hill") and מְגִדּוֹן (*Megiddon*). Thus, the term used in Revelation means "the mountain (or hill) of

Megiddon." This first-century Jewish letter invokes the powerful imagery of this place in foreshadowing a time when Gentile kings would be decisively defeated by Israel's God through the Jewish Messiah (Christ). Like many passages in Revelation, this statement includes a subversive reference to the Roman empire. Through God's judgment the great (and threatening) Roman empire would soon cease to exist.

Who are the Seven Spirits?

In Revelation 1:4-5a we read:

"John, to the seven assemblies located in Asia: Grace to you and peace, from Him who is and who was and who is to come, and from the seven spirits who are before His throne, and from Jesus the Messiah, the faithful witness, the firstborn of the dead, and the ruler of the kings of the earth."

Are these seven spirits before the throne of God really one Holy Spirit? One traditional interpretation connects the seven spirits of Revelation with the seven "aspects" of the Spirit in Isaiah 11:2:

"The Spirit of the LORD will rest on him, the spirit of wisdom and understanding, the spirit of counsel and strength, the spirit of knowledge and fear of the LORD." (NASB)

When counted properly we find only six aspects, not seven, because the Spirit of the Lord should not be understood as one of the aspects of the Spirit of the Lord. A better translation, however, provided by the NET translators, rightly points out that each pair really forms one concept, thus reducing 6 to 3: The Lord's spirit will rest on him – a spirit that gives extraordinary wisdom, a spirit that provides the ability to execute plans, a spirit that produces absolute loyalty to the LORD. (You can see that the count here does not amount to seven at all.)

Second, in non-canonical Jewish books such as 1 Enoch, we find many references to Jewish Son of Man traditions, in which we repeatedly encounter an otherwise unfamiliar phrase, "the Lord of Spirits." For example, we read in 1 Enoch 46:1-2:

"There I beheld the Ancient of Days, whose head was like white wool, and with him another, whose countenance resembled that of a man… Then I inquired of one of the angels, who went with me, and who showed me every secret thing, concerning this Son of Man: who he was; whence he was; and why he accompanied the Ancient of Days. He answered and said to me, This is the Son of Man, to whom righteousness belongs; with whom righteousness has dwelt; and who will reveal all the treasures of that which is concealed: for the Lord of Spirits has chosen him; and his portion has surpassed all before the Lord of Spirits in everlasting uprightness."

This common phrase found in the book of Enoch – "the Lord of Spirits" – may possibly be connected with the "seven spirits who are before his throne" found in Revelation (Rev. 1:4b).

As an interesting side note, the technical term "Holy Spirit" appears in many (sectarian) writings found in the Dead Sea Scroll collection. The Dead Sea Scrolls predate by several hundred years the New Testament writings, which employ the term "Holy Spirit" freely, suggesting a presumed full acceptance of the notion among its audience. In the New Testament the Holy Spirit is described as a powerful and personal force working with Israel's God and His Messiah.

Moreover, a third interpretive possibility presents itself when we once again compare the book of Revelation to 1 Enoch. We could also see the seven spirits as equivalent to seven angelic figures who serve before the throne of God. As evidence for this interpretation, seven such heavenly beings appear not only in the book Enoch, but also in other Jewish books – both Biblical and para-biblical.

While one may be tempted to make too much of this connection, it is important to maintain a certain perspective. The main point is not whether the names of the seven key angels are in fact Gabriel, Michael, Raphael, Uriel, Raquel, Remiel, and Saraquel, as stated in the book of Enoch. Rather, we can say with some reasonable certainty that other contemporary Jews held similar views. This would include John, the Jewish author of the book of Revelation, when he wrote of the seven spirits before the throne of God (cf. 1 Enoch 20:1-8). In so doing, John may have described the Heavenly Court assembled and ready to act:

Israel's God, His anointed Messiah, and the seven powerful angelic beings send a message of both hope and challenge to the first-century followers of the Jewish Christ who struggled under much pressure to find their social identity in the unapologetic and forceful polytheistic Roman society (Rev. 1:4-5).

THE HEBREW LANGUAGE AND JEWISH CULTURE

The Challenge of Translation

Biblical translations obscure the fact that some original wordings in Hebrew present challenges and cannot always be translated with certainty. We the readers are then left unaware that even faithful and hardworking translators must make difficult decisions from several available options suggested by the original text.

Gen. 25:23 is one example of this kind of challenge that translators often face.

"Two nations are in your womb, and two separate peoples shall issue from your body; One people shall be mightier than the other, and the older shall serve the younger."

Translated literally, we read: "Two peoples are in your stomach" – שְׁנֵי גֹיִים בְּבִטְנֵךְ. "Two peoples will be separated from you" – וּשְׁנֵי לְאֻמִּים מִמֵּעַיִךְ יִפָּרֵדוּ. "One people over another will exercise strength – וּלְאֹם מִלְאֹם יֶאֱמָץ. But the last portion of this verse introduces a considerable ambiguity – וְרַב יַעֲבֹד צָעִיר. Traditional translations render it as "the older will serve the younger."

If we really should understand the phrase as "the older will serve the younger," then for some reason the definite articles, as well as the word את (*et*), which marks a direct object, are missing before צָעִיר. Without את the sentence lacks clarity. Perhaps the younger will serve the older; or, as liturgical Jewish singing practice implies, the other way around!

(Another uncertainty is posed by the fact that the opposite of "young" צָעִיר is "old," not "great" רַב as in the Hebrew verse!)

The Biblical texts can indeed present great challenges, and we must make responsible translation decisions even when the text in Hebrew clearly contains a built-in ambiguity. But could it be that the necessity of the translator to choose just one version obscures something more complex that the author intentionally left in the text? Probably so.

Can Work Be Worship?

Adam was given a holy duty – to work the ground. The Hebrew text tells us that Adam himself was created from the very ground he was now commissioned to work. In Hebrew the word for "ground" is אֲדָמָה (*adamah*), and the name of the first human is אָדָם (*adam*). Thus in Hebrew one actually sees and hears the connection between the words *adam* and *adamah*, the one taken from the ground and the ground itself.

Several different words in Hebrew communicate the idea of "worship." One of these words appears in Genesis in the context of God commanding Adam to work the ground in the Garden of Eden. This is the Hebrew word עֲבוֹדָה (*avodah*). Though often translated as "work," it can also be understood as "service" or even "worship." In fact, the same word is used to describe the work of Israel's priests in the tabernacle and temple.

So was Adam's assignment work or worship? Both. Serving God is work, but there is a reason that the word is also translated as "service" and "worship." When God tasked Adam with working the ground in the Garden of Eden, this labor was not yet something affected by sin and death. It was not mere struggle for survival. Adam's work of taking care of God's creation was both his job and his service, his worship.

The Biblical Hebrew Compass

In Genesis 13:14 we read, "And the LORD said to Abram.... Raise your eyes and look out from where you are, to the north [צָפֹנָה] and south [נֶגְבָּה], to the east [קֵדְמָה] and west [יָמָּה]." The Hebrew words for these four points of the compass are pronounced: *tsefonah* ("north"), *negbah* ("south"), *kedmah* ("east"), and *yamah* ("west"). Nowadays the English words sound like technical navigational terms, but in the extremely physical language of Ancient Hebrew the origin of these words was closely tied to the local geographical environment.

The Hebrew word translated as "to the north," צָפֹנָה *(tsefonah),* is connected to Mt. Tsafon or Zaphon (see Isa. 14:13), now known as Jebel Aqra on the border of Syria and Turkey. This mountain lay to Abram's north when God told him to look in all directions.

The Hebrew word נֶגְבָּה *(negbah)*, traditionally translated as "to the south," literally means "to the Negev." This refers to the name of a desert wilderness in the south of the land of Canaan/Israel.

The expression יָמָּה *(yamah)*, translated as "to the west," literally means "to the sea." This refers to the Mediterranean.

Finally, קֵדְמָה *(kedmah)*, translated as "to the east," evokes an image of "going back to something from an earlier time." Its root is connected to the idea of "antiquity" or the distant past. From a Biblical perspective, this suggests the Garden of Eden that God planted "in the east" at the beginning of history (Gen. 2:8).

Someone put it very well: "To read the Bible always and only in translation is like listening to Bach always and only played on the harmonica. You will certainly get the tune, but you will miss pretty much everything else."

The Hebrew Hallelujah

There might not be a single person alive in the Judeo-Christian world who isn't familiar with the word *Hallelujah*. We've all heard this word repeated time and again in various contexts. This word was adopted from Hebrew; in English it is called a Hebrew loan word. But what does this word mean in Hebrew?

The word "Hallelujah" (הַלְלוּיָהּ) is actually two Hebrew words put together, *hallelu* (הַלְלוּ) and *Yah* (יָהּ). We call these compound words. The first word, *hallelu*, is literally an exhortation to praise someone or something, addressed to more than one person (a plural "you"). The old English translation "Praise ye" is therefore accurate. The second component, *Yah*, is an abbreviated version of יהוה (or YHWH in English transliteration), the covenant name of Israel's God.

Some Jewish belief holds that this Name is too holy to be pronounced at all. Moreover, today no one knows how to pronounce it correctly. Early Hebrew writing (and even most modern Hebrew writing) did not use vowels, but only consonants. Most translators, both Jewish and Christian, substitute the word "LORD" instead of trying to reconstruct the pronunciation. This is a rough translation of another Hebrew name for God (אֲדֹנָי, pronounced *Adonai*).

The capital letters used in LORD signify that this is not a translation of the Hebrew word for "Lord," but rather a stand-in for Hebrew YHWH. In Jewish tradition people have also used substitute words to refer to this most holy name of God for centuries: for example, *HaShem* (meaning simply "the

Name") or *Ha-Kadosh Barukh Hu* ("The Holy One, Blessed Be He").

Today many Christ-followers continue to use the translation *LORD*, while others prefer to attempt pronunciations of the actual name YHWH (forbidden in Rabbinic Judaism). Still others use traditional Jewish substitutes for the Name of God or yet another means of expressing their devotion. Regardless of our personal opinions and practices, we should value the search for much-needed authenticity and originality in faithful living. In one way or another, we should affirm the Israelite roots and character of our modern prayers without losing sight of the graciousness of Israel's God, who is far more concerned with our hearts than our grammar.

What Does Prayer Mean in Hebrew?

In the English language, prayer is largely defined by the idea of asking. In earlier English, one could say, either to God or to anyone else: "I pray thee to do such and such." The basic concept here expresses a heart-felt request. However, the Jewish concept of prayer, which comes from the Hebrew word תפילה (*tefilah*), reflects a different type of interaction.

The primary meaning of the verb להתפלל (*lehitpalel*), from which we derive the noun, is a sense of self-judgement or introspection. Particularly in later Jewish Hassidic traditions, *tefilah* embodies an introspection that results in a bonding between the created being and the Creator, as a child would bond with his/her father. This remains true even when requests are involved.

Thus, it comes as no surprise that when Jesus' disciples inquired how they should pray, the Jewish Christ taught them to address their Heavenly King as "Our Father" (Matt. 6:9). We must understand that every one of Jesus' words carry significance, because shortly before this instruction He warned them to avoid using vain repetitions that characterized pagan approaches to prayer (Matt. 6:7).

In another example, we find a curious phrase in Isaiah 56:7: "These I will bring to My holy mountain, and make them joyful in the house of My prayer" (וְשִׂמַּחְתִּים בְּבֵית תְּפִלָּתִי). Note the wording here: instead of "My house of prayer," as in most translations, it can be understood as "the house of My prayer" (cf. Babylonian Talmud, Berakhot 7A). But how is it possible for God to engage in prayer? And with whom?

The answer lies in understanding that Hebrew prayer consists not only of a "request-making session." Rather it reflects a communal bonding between God and His child. Therefore, the house of "His prayer" represents the place where God Himself engages in introspection and sharing and in so doing bonds deeply with His people. They in turn reciprocate this action in their own prayers and bond with Him.

What We Think We Know

A wise person once said, "We are most blinded not by what we don't know, but by what we think we do know." Take, for example, some words we freely use today – "church" and "synagogue." As everyone knows, a/the "church" is a Christian institution, while a/the "synagogue" is a Jewish institution. Right? Well… not really. That is what the words mean today, but things were very different in the first century.

The word translated as *church* is the Ancient Greek word *ekklesia,* which basically means a body of people united by some purpose. In the first century there was nothing specifically Christian about this term or its meaning. Therefore, it is simply inaccurate to translate this word today as "church." A more appropriate word would be "assembly" or "gathering" (see, for example, Rev. 1:20-2:1).

Similarly, the word usually translated as *synagogue* also did not have an exclusively Jewish meaning. "Synagogues" were places where people gathered for meetings in the Greco-Roman world – often places where anyone could come and engage in community activities. Jews certainly made extensive use of this institution, but even in "synagogues of the Jews" other people also participated (see, for example, Acts 15:21).

Customary NT translations render the Ancient Greek word *sunagoge* with a neutral English word like *assembly* or *congregation* only when it appears in a positive context (e.g., James 2:2). However, when the context seems to be negative, the same translations use *synagogue* instead – as in the infamous passage about the "synagogue of Satan" (Rev. 3:9). Conversely, *ekklesia* is translated as *church* only in positive contexts, but by neutral words in negative contexts (e.g., Acts 19:41).

This practice not only changes the meaning of the original texts, but it also makes almost every bad assembly sound "Jewish" and almost every good assembly sound "Christian." When we notice such biases in our translations, we should at the very least stop and think and reconsider!

Grace in Judaism

The Jewish prayer book, the *Siddur* (a word that means "order" in Hebrew), developed over many centuries to help worshipers offer prayers to God in a way consistent with the teachings of the Torah and other sacred literature.

In one place, the Siddur directs every Jew to include in their daily prayers the following words (based on Daniel 9:18):

> רִבּוֹן כָּל הָעוֹלָמִים
> לֹא עַל צִדְקֹתֵינוּ אֲנַחְנוּ מַפִּילִים תַּחֲנוּנֵינוּ לְפָנֶיךָ כִּי עַל רַחֲמֶיךָ הָרַבִּים
>
> "Master of all worlds,
> It is not on the basis of our righteousness that we lay our requests before Your presence, but because of Your great mercies."

This prayer (among many others) illustrates that the Judaism which emerged after the destruction of Temple in 70 C.E. continued to uphold this basic Jewish teaching about human action and divine mercy. Keeping the commandments of God, although very important, does not form the basis for God's compassion toward His people.

The apostle Paul, expecting a positive response, reminded Peter that it was common knowledge among the Jews that Torah observance alone did not provide the basis for right standing before God. In so doing, he challenged Peter to accept Gentile God-fearers who believed in the Jewish Christ as citizens in the

Kingdom of God alongside Jews, without the need for a proselyte conversion.

We read in Gal. 2:15-16:

"We are Jews by birth and not sinners from among the Gentiles. We know that a man is not justified by the works of the Torah, but through faith in the Messiah Jesus…"

The modern Jewish Siddur, therefore, shares with the Jewish apostle Paul a common understanding that the basis for relationship with God is not just keeping the Torah (no matter how wonderful and good it is!), but rather the grace and mercy of Israel's God.

Thank You for Not Making Me a Woman

Every religious Orthodox Jewish male recites as part of his daily prayer: "Blessed are you, LORD our God, Ruler of the Universe, who has not made me a woman." Prior to this blessing he also blesses God for not making him "a Gentile" or "a slave." To many people these statements conclusively prove Judaism's anti-Gentile and anti-female posture. But is this conclusion correct?

While God gave the entire Torah specifically to Israel, many of its important laws concerned the nations as well. But even within Israel, certain laws applied differently to different groups (men, women, priests, Levites, kings, and slaves, among others).

Even though God commanded the nations to obey certain laws in the Torah, they were not responsible for observing the same number of commandments as the people of Israel.
Therefore, the blessing thanking God for "not making me a Gentile" does not reflect Jewish superiority, but rather indicates a ready and willing attitude to obey a greater number of commandments. The same principle applies in the case of women and slaves.

The apostle Paul (Shaul) taught that the Torah's laws were never designed as a mechanism for placing anyone in a position of right standing before Israel's God. He argued that with the coming of King Jesus, the inclusion of Gentiles within the membership of God's people had to follow the original Israelite method, as demonstrated in Abraham's justification by grace through faith. Abraham believed God; then he was declared righteous, and only then was he circumcised (Gen. 15:1-6; Rom. 4:1-3; Gen. 17).

Based on this context from the Torah, Paul explained how Gentiles can become full members of God's family – belonging to the Jewish Christ without proselyte conversion.

"There is neither Jew nor Greek [Gentile], there is neither slave nor free man, there is neither male nor female; for you are all one in Christ Jesus. And if you belong to Christ, then you are Abraham's descendants, heirs according to promise" (Gal. 2:27-28).

In comparing the Jewish prayer with Paul's statement, we remarkably note that they not only mention the same three groups (Jews/Gentiles, slaves/freemen, men/women), but even use the same order! Among other points, this comparison shows that some modern Jewish traditions trace their roots back to the first century, and also that the apostle Paul wrote his letters to the nations from within Judaism, not outside of it.

Benjamin Netanyahu's Name

Israel's latest elections occurred in 2015, resulting in Benjamin Netanyahu retaining his position as prime minister after a heated campaign. Both supporters and proponents of "Bibi" wanted the new government to face and meet the various challenges the country faces.

Just for the record: I voted for another candidate, because I believed that Israel was in need of a different direction than the one promoted by Benjamin Netanyahu and his cabinet. However, I accept the result of our democratic elections. I hope the current government will be committed to building a stronger and better Israel for all of its citizens and residents, in the hope that one day we will be able to live in peace with our neighbors.

In honoring the office of prime minister, I would like to discuss the Hebrew meaning of the name *Benjamin Netanyahu*. Even today Israeli names often have deep meanings, which are linked to Biblical history.

Grammatically speaking, *Benjamin* (בִּנְיָמִן) is a compound word comprised of two elements, *ben* and *yamin*. *Ben* (בֵּן) means "son," while *yamin* (יָמִין) means "right hand" (or the direction "right"). Thus the basic meaning of the name *Benjamin* is "son of the right hand" (see Gen. 35:18).

Netanyahu (נְתַנְיָהוּ) is also a compound word, made up of the elements *natan* and *yahu*. The word *natan* (נָתַן) means "he gave," while *Yahu* (יָהוּ) is a shortened version of the proper name of the God of Israel (יהו or YHWH). So if we were to translate the current prime minister's last name, it would mean something like "YHWH gave." (The name of the city *Netanyah* in central Israel shares these two roots with *Netanyahu*).

It is very important to learn the basics of Hebrew. Once you do, you will discover riches of the Hebrew Bible (Old Testament) that you have not yet imagined. As a modern Christ-follower you have become an heir to the great faith of Abraham, Isaac, and Jacob, alongside the Jewish people. This means that the language of Israel is also part of your heritage! Own it. Learn it. Enjoy it!

Made in the
USA
Columbia, SC